A QUESTION OF SEEING

A QUESTION OF SEEING

Poems by Donald Finkel

THE UNIVERSITY OF ARKANSAS PRESS
FAYETTEVILLE 1998

02   01   00   99   98   5   4   3   2   1

Text designed by Ellen Beeler
Jacket designed by Liz Lester

☉ The paper used in this publication meets the minimum requirements of the American
National Standard for Permanence of Paper for Printed Library Materials Z39.48-1984.

LIBRARY OF CONGRESS CATALOGING-IN-PUBLICATION DATA

Finkel, Donald.
        A question of seeing : poems / by Donald Finkel.
             p.   cm.
        ISBN 1-55728-501-2 (alk. paper). — ISBN 1-55728-502-0 (pbk. : alk. paper)
        I. Title.
        PS3556.I48Q47   1998
        811'.54—dc21   97-39771
                                                                    CIP

For Constance, *malgré tout*

Acknowledgments

Some of these poems, or versions thereof, have appeared in *Antaeus, Best American Poetry 1995, Borderlands, Chicago Review, Denver Quarterly, Grand Street, Kenyon Review, Manhattan Review, New England Review, Ontario Review, Pacific Review, Paris Review, Poetry, River Styx, Sagarin Review, San Miguel Writer, Seneca Review, Southwest Review, Tapas,* and *Yale Review.* Versions of some passages in "What Comes to a Man" first appeared in *The Detachable Man.*

Contents

❧ 1 ❧

IN THE CLEARING

One

Independence Day (while for us the bugle sounds retreat).
Down in the schoolyard the fathers are offloading rockets
whereas off to the left a pile driver hasn't quit yet,
an implacable *whap whap* of the hammer, a drumfire of progress.
At the tip of each quivering dendrite dance ten thousand angels
brandishing rapiers or strumming molecular harps.

Here in the clearing, hemmed in by honeysuckle,
beleaguered by insults and promises, tocsins and prophecies,
switchblades and pheromones swarming at every pore—
it's keep treading, private, to pause is to drown.
Surrounded by windflower, speedwell, sweet yellow clover,
we can let the angels enter one at a time.

Few weeds are tolerant of shade. It was man who opened the sunny spots where weeds are happiest.

How good to be back at headquarters, back at the threshold
between the labyrinth and the wilderness, one chaos and another,
where mornings are sunny, evenings pensive, nights incontestable.
How grand to greet the neighbors again by name,
on speaking terms with ragweed and sow thistle,
skullcap, burdock, bitterroot, and nettle,
intimate, familiar, thick as thieves.
Time was, I made way for my cohorts,
slashing and burning from here to the capital
without respite, without reflection.
How sweet to be home again with my people,
a consummate, sovereign, irresistible weed.

Sundance the cat will no doubt be your first concern, as he will insist upon being fed.

     Who is this dark lover come calling, this inky maharajah
     behind whom the underbrush is a palisade
     of blackberry and goldenrod? Black as the lips of silence,
     it's Sundance, strolling his minimalist grove,
     fifteen red maples and three white pines,
     eighteen dryads dancing on the barbered grass,
     a three-dimensional frieze on an animate urn.
     He called this morning with a gift in his mouth—
     a vole, clasping and unclasping the shadow
     in its elf-grey hand. Who's feeding whom?
     What's Sundance's first concern? Unsettling
     how much (the front door shut between us)
     his cry of triumph sounded like a howl of pain.

What things so ever ye desire, when ye pray, believe that ye receive them and ye shall have them.

     Reviewing the troops on the shelves of the upstairs study:
     Have You Felt Like Giving Up Lately? Are You Confused?
     The Hunger for Reality. I can all but savor
     the tang of the owner's convictions wafting from the pages.
     Penciled in the margin of *How to Pray:*
     Prayers of two or more, when feeling
     the same burden, are very strong.
     And down in the living room, *Living in Step,*
     Hey, I'm Alive! The Total Woman, The Book of Trees—
     and what have we brought for sustenance?
     One copy of *Chaos* and two *Rogets.*

All the plants will need watering. I will probably leave a few in the kitchen sink.

    In baskets, basins, clay pots, plastic,
    garden soil, potting soil, vermiculite, water,
    huddled on benches, railings, tables,
    lurking on windowsills, dangling from rafters,
    blooming, drooping, lush, tubercular,
    some under the weather (such as there is in here),
    some bushy-tailed, fresh as a hothouse daisy—
    yet all of them docile, self-deprecating,
    hushed and trusting as if they were
    expecting us (housebroken like them),
    rich kin from the interior.

The pond looks pretty only after a big rain storm. There are apparently no underground springs, despite what the builder told me.

    Some pond—a crater in the grass with a bed of dusty mud tiles
    flaunting that valance of lavender mimulus,
    a sort of dysfunctional rain trap, a brontosaurus print,
    an old war wound. And above, closing in on every side,
    that siege of horsemint and heal-all, speedwell, skullcap,
    and wild marjoram, flourishing pennants of purple and blue,
    closing in like a legion of militant weeds.

    Sundance is cutting through the maples, reconnoitering,
    appraising with his pale-green non-Euclidean eye
    the lay of the land. Now he steps from the shadow
    and lets the trees get on with it, reading the future

with their clairvoyant roots, praying to the dark star
at the heart of their darkness. Sunlight leaps
from his flank, a fusillade of shooting stars.

§

Walden is blue at one time and green another, even from the same point of view.

Last night's rain has beaten the mimulus flat as a blanket,
the floor of the pond is weeds from shore to shore,
ripples of joe-pye weed and wild marjoram,
ghost-minnows of violet and lavender winking and flickering.
If I'd a mind, I'd walk across it.

§

Strange bird haranguing us from the evening wood,
one three-note measure echoed relentlessly
till even our obstinate hearts begin pounding in triplets.

Two

At the boundary, life blossoms.

This evening an apparition: a half-grown doe
emerging from the maples, sniffing and peering,
skirting the boundary, seeking a way out
as if our clearing were merely one bad patch
in some incomprehensible counterpane,
the breeze that kissed the dew from the dayflower's lips
one whiff of the whirlwind, one tatter
of that inscrutable turbulence we call weather.
At last the doe leaps over a clump of skullcap,
vanishing as eerily as she appeared, leaving
under the half-wild apple a cloud of gnats.
Not every cloud has a silver lining.

§

Bright red slash from the pine to the sumacs.
By the time you can say *cardinal,* he's gone,
lost in that rabble of green shadows next door.

§

And the builder said, Let there be clearing,
and behold! there was clearing up and clearing out,
there was lopping and cropping, there was
leveling and laying bare (save fifteen maples
and three half-grown pines spared by the builder's dozer).
And lo! an opening, a respite, a let-up, a breather,
a break in the chaos, an island of tentative order
in a sea of disorder, absolution, acquittal, reprieve.

§

Our horizon is never quite at our elbows. The thick wood is not just at our door, nor the pond, but somewhat is always clearing, familiar and worn by us, appropriated and fenced in some way, and reclaimed from Nature.

Down by the spruce a little crowd of weed-trees
squints in the morning light. It's sumac, stealing
from the selvage—*Rhus.* Some say from *rheo,* I run.
(A little clearing in time. No time to rest.
Just time to re-group, our nerves at full alert,
to rally the battle-scarred, call up the reserves.)

§

Jerry the lawn-man grins from the riding mower
like a tanker from his turret. He's retaken the clearing.
The spindling sumac grove lies lopped and scattered.
This spring, Jerry says, he took his kid mountain climbing.

The little shaver's weed-whacking the timothy.
One reckless bead of sweat rappels down his brow.

§

Sundance has dropped another jewel on our stoop,
the head of a chipmunk cleanly severed, the tiniest
wound at the throat where a little life keeps oozing out.

§

*. . . a butterfly stirring the air today in Peking can transform storm systems next month in
New York.*

We keep circling back like the lost
or the enchanted. Circling the thicket of memory,
we back into a clearing, fetch up by a windless pond
trembling like the doe, sniffing and peering.
One quivering leaf on that maple might set off a storm
in its hippocampus. One breath from our lips might send
a mower hurtling through this nursery of infant sumacs.
Not leviathan but a butterfly engages the gears of creation.

§

Sort of a sortie, slipping past the outposts of abandon.
Under the pines, a family of raspberry blossoms
smiling behind their broad green hands. I draw one closer
to inspect. Like rubbing my finger on a slave girl's teeth.

§

After the rain, like homeless men from under a bush,
the slugs creep onto the flags to sun themselves
while Thoreau's unwashed ghost shuffles through the maples,

past the woodshed, pausing at the mulch pail
(that furnace of decay) to warm his heart.

I confess that I have hitherto indulged very little in philanthropic enterprises.

Asked on his deathbed what he thought of the world to come:
One world at a time, he croaked, as deep in their sockets
the grey eyes flared that incandescent blue
like bolts of chicory blazing in the roadside dust.
One pond, one plot, one thimbleful of this world
offered that pinchpenny eremite quite enough,
who built his house from the boards of a squatter's shack.

I had to pay four dollars and twenty-five cents tonight, he to vacate at five tomorrow morning . . .

with his wife and his bawling four-month daughter—
the infant Fitchburg Railroad (that last improvement)
having no further need of their services.

At six I passed him and his family on the road. One large bundle held their all,—bed, coffee-mill, looking-glass, hens,—all but the cat, she took to the woods

—which offered her barely enough of this world, or the next
(having yielded the last of her lives in a woodchuck trap).
No room at the pond for the luxury of guilt.

. . . if I repent of any thing, it is very likely to be my good behavior.

THREE

The purpose of an orchestra
        is to organize those sounds
               and hold them
to an assembled order   .
        in spite of the
               "wrong note."

Deep in the pit the pond lays down a ground bass,
a drone of invisible bees. Out by the road
the chicory is crooning its indigo blues.
The catbird chimes in with a clumsy fugue,
never stumbling over the same note twice,
only a cat in quotes that black gnats hover round
as if to say "not quite." With that little black cap
it seems less like a song than a call to prayer.

I do have a compost pile behind the woodshed. If you feel so inclined.

Raking the hummock of compost down to the quick,
watching the pillbug skitter, the centipede race,
the termite lug her wings through the steaming humus,
the slug wave his glistening palps in the emptiness,
we saw the granddaddy of earthworms haul himself
laboriously like a wounded titan from the abyss,
a gash in his side from which the rancor leaked,
where the teeth of the rake sank through like the fangs of chaos.

It's time to shovel fresh greens down the throat of decay,
this morning's orange peel onto last year's beets,
winding diaphanous corn silk round ash-grey cobs,
scrambling the seasons, damn the stratigraphy,
tearing a hole in the darkness to let in the day.

Nothing but Sundance and myself, against
the cannonry of chaos, nothing to flourish
but our fine intentions. He armed to the teeth,
I with my *Who's Who of Weeds,*
marshaling the troops, inspecting the earthworks.

Nothing but the great black hunter and me
marching to the pipes of the border guard.

No tilling, dibbling, mulching, pruning,
plowing, planting, reaping, gleaning,
harrows, combines, herbicides—
save, every other Monday, one
weed whip and one riding mower,
only that momentary setback.
Then Tuesday morning the weeds crank up
their tiny engines and resume
their mild affectionate forays.

No digging sticks, no fertility rites,
only the two of us now and then
tending our own improbable garden,
scattering in a rented bed
doubtful seed on dubious ground.
Then strolling out through that glorious crop
of plantain, yarrow, chickweed, bedstraw,
skullcap, heal-all, cinquefoil, sorrel,
fertilized with nothing more
or less than our unlikely love.

A white flash in the upper branches of the aspen,
a rataplan of leaves—and who should float down
onto the new-mown lawn but a red-tailed hawk
to shake out his ominous, archangelic wings,
baring those improbable pantaloons.

This system was robust. If you perturbed it slightly, as any natural system is slightly per-turbed by noise, the strangeness would not go away.

Small noise, the snarl of the mower, the catbird's mew,
the robin's mantra: *me! me! me!*
addressed to whomever it might concern.
(There are, after all, other systems yet more strange
where, should you let the moth of a whisper slip
past your clenched teeth, all is irrevocably lost.)
Strange but robust, robust yet exquisitely strange,
the outlandish biomechanics of the birds,
the maggoty dynamics of a compost pile,
a pond of flowers, a garden lush with weeds.

§

The ants have sent their aphids out to graze
by the pond (on the giddy pasture of a cottonwood leaf)
while the beetles keep munching and humping on the rose
and the sumacs flaunt their unlikely parasols
while Sundance sleeps inside on the easiest chair
and the asters carry on with their weedy amours,
while the bee-balm gossips with a potted fern
through the living-room window and the sun rains down
volley on volley of ultraviolet fire.

§

Sundance comes round to have a word (it sounds like
Now!)—leaps onto the bench, a couple of brotherly jabs
with his head in my ribs, then he settles beside me
to contemplate his kingdom.

§

Not only is it improbable that the "way back" can be found; as speciation increases, the possibility decreases that any new route can be found . . .

Time to pack up our tiny allotment of chaos,
time to retreat in earnest, time to go home,
for turbulence breeds its own improbable order
and the way back and ahead are one and the same.
We take our clearings when and where we find them,
and leave them when we go to their own devices,
a few gifts pressed in a book like schoolgirl keepsakes,
dried and flattened, etiolated, priceless.

2

FOUR PORTRAITS OF THE ARTIST AS AN OLD MAN

1: PICASSO'S APHRODITE FOR ALBERTI

To brighten the irises of the young Alberti,
his erstwhile exile-in-arms (barely sixty-six),
Picasso runs the tip of his brush along
the Willendorfian rondure of her breasts.
They rise beneath her arms like beatified moons
as she draws her fingers through her seaweed hair.

Now his moist brush plunges down the sheer
Minoan waist; now, wafted on thermals,
caresses the eloquent haunches, twiddles
the starfish nipples in the grip of this
incorrigible eighty-six-year-old satyr;
now strokes in passing (like an afterthought)
the tiny equivocal face; now bids his comrade
farewell beneath one spectacular satellite:
Su amigo Picasso 8.1.68.

2: MONDRIAN: VICTORY BOOGIE-WOOGIE

Mondrian is said, as he grew old, to have invariably sat with his back to the window because the sight of trees . . . filled him with revulsion.

Seventy-two years tilting at the windmills
of the actual. Seventy-two years keeping
chaos at bay, reclaiming artifice
by inches from the encroaching sea.

Seventy-two years promising an earthly paradise—
"if only our intentions are good enough
it should not prove impossible": trees
true as plumb lines, a dancer naked, slender,
proud as a tower, an odalisque

serene as the low unbroken Dutch horizon,
outstretched like a seamless levee. (Not to mention
a couple of desperately ideal cityscapes,
besotted with Broadway, "where the mathematical-
artistic temperament of the future"
should be rendered incarnate.)

And still at his back through the window something
was silently writhing, fluttering, plunging.
Soon enough he'd be a flat one himself. And the year
after that (how could he imagine?) the mathematicians
would demonstrate the dead-on-the-level logic
of $E=mc^2$ over Hiroshima.

3: DUCHAMP DESCENDING STAIRCASE

Midwinter, midnight, striding into the wind
across Union Square between the naked trees,
he conjures behind the façades battalions of wheels
turning wearily on their stools.

If only he could cease this restless descent,
the stairs would bear him backwards like an escalator,
sliding between glossy pages off a thousand coffee tables.
Yet he persists, an idea who's long outlived his time,
an androgynous Alice avalanching down
his private rabbit hole, to stay in place,
swimming against a torrent of good taste,
straining to leave no wake.

Already his porcelain *Fountain* is creeping
down the museum stairs to stand on her head
in the gentlemen's lavatory. Already
his faultless marble sugar cubes are pirouetting
into the delft-blue bowls of the bourgeoisie.

He's been preparing now for twenty years,
assembling even as he turns westward along 14th
the elements of one last scream of the peacock
he calls *Given:* twin peepholes in a wooden door
through which one voyeur at a time
can peer at the beaver of the Lady with the Gas Lamp
(his rendition of that elusive angel, Liberty),
asprawl on the shore of a picture-postcard lake
set off by authentic twigs and a waterfall.

4: FIGURE AND GROUND

I draw with scissors.

A snapshot of Matisse in bed at Le Rêve,
near the end of the book, though there are still
a few last pages. He's working on one right now.
A shape is coming free from the square in his hand,
from time, fatigue, old age, from the wounded body
of France, of Europe, Earth, the universe.
The wall behind him teems with enchanted beasts,
with nudes like flowers, stars like birds, two ferns
tending a paper fire like a sacrifice.

Yet he is never so mesmerized by the shape
that he has forgotten the absence that remains,
the lineaments of vacancy and loss:
the silhouette on a dingy, down-drawn shade
of the pensioner gumming his gruel, the remorseless smile
on the torturer's lips as he tightens the screw, or the cool
compassionate dark into which the prisoner descends,
or that composition down in the kitchen yard
where the garbage men are heaving onto their wagon
dove-grey cinders blazoned with tangerine rind,
the leavings of Le Rêve, nor so swept up
by his paper phrases that he has forgotten the voice

from which they were pared, or the shape that's left unsaid,
not only the scraps of insight, but the vast
ignorance from which they spring, nor grown
so giddy waltzing with those delectable sisters
Figure and Ground that he has forgotten the edges
cutting their way through the uncomplaining paper.

THREE STANDARD STOPPAGES
(Marcel Duchamp)

1:

We shall determine the conditions for the instantaneous state of Rest (or allegorical appearance) of a succession . . . of various facts, seeming to necessitate each other under certain laws, in order to isolate the sign of the accordance between, on the one hand, this state of Rest (capable of all the innumerable eccentricities) and, on the other, a choice of Possibilities authorized by these laws . . .

> Duchamp measures out and emancipates with his razor
> one meter's worth of bleached white cotton thread,
> then fixes the ends in a pair of surgical clamps
> one meter precisely above a bed of wet plaster,
> horizontal, taut, in a "state of Rest"—
> then releases the meter, so that it falls "as it pleases"
> (though under certain unalterable laws
> of threadness, meterhood, and gravity),
> to arrive at a postlapsarian state of Rest,
> caught in the act, a snapshot of abandon—
> an effect so eccentric and so necessary,
> the creator arranges a second fall to grace,
> then a third for good measure, that the threads recline,
> three odalisques on the complaisant plaster,
> tricked out in nothing but Possibility.

The 3 standard stoppages are the meter diminished.

> At last, with a smile and the faintest "touch of malice,"
> Duchamp restores to the geometer
> his previously irreproachable meters,
> diminished and immortalized at once,
> lounging on their plaster of Paris divan.

2:

Buy a dictionary and cross out the words to be crossed out. Sign: revised and corrected.

    Like coins worn smooth with commerce, clipped and shaved,
    debased, ablated, thinner than paper, the words
    have lost their savor, floating in the air between us,
    spent breath, faint exhalations, scentless gusts:
    it's time for a pinch of salt, a soupçon of savory.

    Like a stone some thirsty traveler might suck
    to soothe his tongue, a noun squats in the clearing,
    an oblate sphere, pointless, opaque,
    useless as tits on a boar. Flat on its back,
    a verb is waving its wasted legs in the leaflight.

    Here in the jungle of grammar, dozing like a sloth,
    flaccid and bland as a custard apple, it's time
    for a clove of minced irony, a gust of fresh gusto,
    some gesture, flourish, arabesque of breath,
    chink of sunlight in the leafage, parrot-scream.

3:

Establish a society in which the individual has to pay for the air he breathes (air meters; imprisonment and rarefied air in case of non-payment, simple asphyxiation if necessary . . .)

    Drafted, a factory-fresh constitution in the country
    of the Ready-Made, a century ahead of time.
    Hot off the press, a new bureaucracy—
    commissions, councils, boards, directorates,
    undersecretaries, periwigged magistrates—

Ministry of Coincidences.
Department, or better,
Regime of Coincidence.
Ministry of Gravity.

I've forgotten again to ask the glass for water.
Here it is at my place, half empty as ever.
And how many years has it been since I knelt to the carpet,
praised a window or applauded a door,
lit one candle for the soul of a castoff shoe?

I've exhausted the talent of pencils, the patience of mirrors,
drained the reservoir of repentance. It was I
who depleted the treasury of wonder, with never a thought
for the consequences. I promise, I'll begin tomorrow
recycling my empty concessions, set about conserving
the angular momentum of daybreak, the urgency of grass,
harnessing the tides of regret, the gravity of grief.
Tomorrow, I give you my word, I'll say grace to the glass.

A QUESTION OF SEEING

It's a question of seeing
so much clearer,

of doing to things
what light does to them.

—*Guillevic*

Softer than thistledown, blind as a mole,
morning creeps through the leafage,
snuffling and nuzzling.

Here, here, it whispers,
clinging to surfaces, a glittering nimbus,
an aureole of breathless quanta.

It's a question of reading the leaves
so gently not even the dust is discomposed.
Not even the breeze has so light a caress.

If only words were as light-fingered,
stealing through the underbrush, leaving
not the faintest trace,

if only words were as weightless, as imponderable,
skimming the discourse of grass,
that tremulous braille.

CONCERNING THE WINDOW

How much has the window left to give?

It opens this morning on a prospect drained of ardor
under a heavy slate-grey brow of cloud—
same trees, same fields, same mountains brooding on the horizon,
hands in their pockets, shoulders bowed.

Who's to blame if it never looks out on a sunrise?

Ingenuous, unsleeping, unlike us
it has not chosen this. If it lived
at the bottom of an airshaft it would gaze out every morning
with the same wide-eyed surprise.

Who's to blame if we forget to press our foreheads against it
and see what it sees—

as, after ten thousand nights and more together,
bound loosely, not so much by habit
as by a mild, benign addiction, we wake
beside ourselves as ever?

HIS COLLAR

In the dark woods, on the sodden ground, I found my way only by the whiteness of
his collar.

—*Franz Kafka*

How with that one pallid detail he realizes
an otherwise fabulous wood.

What business had that collar,
you might ask him, in the boscage?

Ask rather what in the world he would do
without that rag of light, his only guide.

Not even moonlight, only that threadbare,
fugitive, twice-reflected gleam.

BOOKS

Long since the commissars buried your history,
scattered grey flowers on the grave.
An army of bureaucrats drank up
your language and spat out dossiers.

Sleepless, you wandered room to room
like pitiful vampires. "We've had our
bellyful of blood," you muttered.
"Only books can fill this emptiness."

Long since we'd grown weary of tropes,
those trivial mirrors, bloodless,
two-dimensional, weightless as pallor,
thinner than onion skin.

So we brought you our books, all we could carry,
and huddled round your tables as you feasted,
warming our hands in the slow fire of discourse,
eyes smarting from the acrid smoke.

PIANO MAN

"Thanks, man," he mumbles as the cabbie
relinquishes his arm, flashing over his shoulder
that incorrigible blindman's smile, a parting shot,
then turns it on me and reaches out his hand.
Clenched around something I can't hope to see,
the blunt, frost-blackened fingers graze my palm,
stiff but oddly civil, a manicured claw.

Two years ago, coldest night of the year,
coming home from a two-bit taproom gig,
the smile froze to his face like a mask of ice.
Snow lay around so thick, he couldn't raise
a peep from the pavement with his radar stick.
A block to the left and two-and-a-half to the right,
then he curled in an alley and slept the sleep of the numb
between nine jiggers of whiskey and the weather.

Lighting up now, he clamps his cancer stick
close to the tip, to steady it for the flame:
incense of smoldering flesh. Can't work his zipper,
asks me, can I wait while he fishes it out
and dribbles over his shoes, to zip him up.

Hard luck pounded a rolling bass on his bones—
but didn't he ramble through the difficult changes.
And doesn't he parry my question with the same damned smile:
"Look, man, blindness is the least of my problems."

WHEN WE OPENED THE DOOR

Skeletal, draggled, a rough draft of a cat,
distended dugs betokening a litter
of moribund kittens under somebody's porch—
when we opened the door that day, love crept in too,

who reigned for years, every inch the queen,
purring long-drawn doxologies of breath,
whetting her claws on our benevolence.
When we opened the door that day, grace crept in too,

who lay of a morning supine on a pallet of sunlight,
four paws to heaven, licking herself into shape,
dreaming her undulant way into old age.
When we opened the door that day, peace crept in too.

Draped tranquilly on the doctor's stainless table,
liquor of oblivion trickling through her veins,
she sighs one final sutra and sends us away.
When we opened the door that day, death crept in too.

SEPTEMBER MORN

The sweetgum stands ankle deep in a pool of leaves,
red-gold, star-sharp, fragrant when crushed.
A hundred leaf-scars lace her scale-grey bark,
bleeding sweet sap wherever a star has fallen.

Come February her bones will still be decked
with dry brown seedballs, prickly to the touch,
baubles from some long-dead holiday—
as if there were something still to celebrate.

THE DISMAL SCIENCE

Like hogs in Iowa sometimes—too much of it now,
and no one's buying. Oh it smelt so of promise,
the great trucks reeked of it, sows bursting with farrow,
the city clamoring, the prices soaring.

In the guts of the city a young man hunches over
a kitchen table, scribbling. His freezer's crammed
with bittersweet elegies, low-salt epigrams.
Poems breed in his larder. He goes on scribbling.

He could pick up an epic this morning
from the take-away rack at the local supermarket.
All over the city young men are scribbling, scribbling,
and old women, and schoolchildren, and several chimpanzees.

The young man persists in his kitchen, parboiling a dithyramb
while the sows go farrowing on in Iowa.
Welcome to the eleventh plague: plenty.
There's room enough in here for everyone.

3

ON THE SHINGLE

Below on the shingle a man's skipping pebbles:
gravely they wait at his feet for another go-round
of scouring and burnishing—
                              slabs of sea-worn granite,
slate leaves, stemless, iridescent, bruised gold wafers,
shards of sea-glass, garnet, amethyst—
                              a mild,
complaisant, saintly rabble, sunning themselves
in the nakedness of their imperfections.

Everywhere he turns, on this stony beach
the tide affords between the pinewood and the briny,
collops and lozenges, arrowheads and amulets,
leap to his hand and hurl themselves
at Odom's Ledge.
                  A moment there I'd have sworn
that one was walking on water.

&

high above, the pinewood, abiding:
balsam and oak-mould, boletus,
armillaria, agaric, inky cap,
a nameless lime-green moss like
the froth of chaos, corpse-pale
Indian Pipe, that blackens at the touch,
the hemlock branch swinging shut
on my passage like a frail green gate

&

The eons have beaten a door in the upthrust slate
the tide saunters through, on his way out:

a brooding lintel, a threshold of dingy granite
I'd just as soon sit on as step over.
Tide's still lapping the threshold while sunlight
toe-dances on a doormat of bladderwrack.

§

tide's going out: kicking their petticoats,
the whitecaps can-can out on Odom's Ledge
as Odom rises from his six-hour soak
with his eight sunbathing harbor seals
and fourteen cormorants, hanging their
dark, tragicomical wings to dry

§

Half the day it's the tide's turn, half the day mine,
going or coming—or what's a doorway for?

§

beyond the door, the empery of seaweed,
greeny-brown furze on the pubes of Atlantis,
patches of beach grass, sprays of sea lavender,
three orphan pools where nothing swims,
an osprey circling, circling, high and,
huddled on the underslung lip of the bluff,
an oak tree, cradling in the crook of one root
the book of slate

§

Boulder squats in the water like a fat old buddha,
nothing showing but the top of his shaven pate.
Erratic, za-zen, up to his elbows in silt,

he's leading the simple life: twice-daily sitz-baths,
plenty of sunlight, moonlight, fresh salt air,
and both feet firmly planted in the grave.

Six hours from now he'll rise, renewed, a crown
of rockweed on his feldspar-freckled dome,
just another igneous hobo passing through,
down by the river, waiting for the ice-age local,
flanked by mile on mile of homeless buddhas
lining both shores, shawls of seaweed
round their shoulders, prayer mats of weed.

§

      wind has his own agenda

§

A supercharged tangerine jolly boat rips down the silence like a self-propelled
chainsaw. Trough on trough, wavelet after wavelet cross and recross as, deep in
its dream, the river whimpers. The boulders croon to it in unison, mile on mile.
Back of every buddha: a tranquil pool, rocking in a seaweed cradle.

§

      love comes to this:
                a long while resting
   side by side, like mica-flecked erratics
   varnished with light, like mossy boulders
   between a sleep and a sleep, as cliff and tide
   spin out their conversation,
                   as a cormorant
   takes off into the wind, dark seraphim,
   beating the water with his wings

§

Lobsterman's dog barks at a loose two-pounder
thrashing the foredeck. Hauling traps, the lobsterman
barks back, their voices tossed on the landward breeze
like gnats of sound.
                        We're all of us hard at it here:
a cormorant retraces the arc of the lobster boat's wake,
checking for discards as the lobsterman works downriver
to check his next trap. Beside me an ant's dismantling
the cliff, single-handed. Toes working in the earth,
naked but for the grey-green crown of leaves,
a brawny oak poises at the brink for a swan dive
onto the shingle.
                    Even daylight's working its way
through the windward doorpost, as the doorway opens,
grain by grain by grain.

§

    tide thrusts his salty tongue down the river's throat

§

The incoming tide's brushing the shingle widdershins, laving the continent's
broken toes. In time the tide relents, and the cliff in its own time. Between: the
shingle, grounds of their accord. A little sweetness trickles into the bay.

§

        sails furled, a white two-master
        laboring seaward against the tide
        while, running before the wind,
        a sister passes upriver, tip of her
        full-bellied spinnaker
        quivering with pleasure

§

Crossing slate city, tenements of slate,
slate back-lots teeming, slate graveyards,
middens of slate,
                    in praise of all things
frangible, mutable, fugitive, shattered,
weathered, worn or torn, in praise of cracks,
fractures, great rifts, infinitesimal fissures,
ablation, transience and decay,
                                    I pause
to piss on the shingle, my thimbleful
of inglorious acid.

§

        tourist waves from a rubberneck launch
        and I, by jiminy, I wave gravely back

§

Far beyond the door, where the cliff leans down to the shingle, lie outposts of
beach grass and sea lavender, though the piney slope is bare of both.

§

        behind a tatter of fluttering rockweed,
        a spot of turbulence wrinkles the skin
        of stillness, as cliff and tide rock to
        and fro, between frailty and passion,
        systole and diastole, and the seal lies down
        with the cormorant on Odom's toe

§

To whom it may concern, I leave
this carton of fossils, this shingle museum,
all things shed, shattered, weather-bitten,
out at elbows, worn to the bone,
cast off, dislocated, dispersed
in an endless blissful diaspora:
1 mussel shell, undone, blue robe
eroding in folds from a pearly shoulder,
1 shiver of milk-blue bottle-glass,
the once-cruel edges softly blunted,
1 wafer of white pine lumber, cleanly sawn.

Yet nothing wholly dead: the barnacles
refuse to loose their hold, the lichen's
breathing still on its tatter of bark,
and the spray of sea lavender. Shrouded
in slate, the iron's not done rusting.
1 spruce cone sprouting on its twig like a
minikin thyrsus, 1 crab carapace, on its back
a brooding, burnt-sienna buddha face.

I can hear the seals tuning up
on Odom's thigh, the gull's *yeeee-ha!*
straddling a vagrant gust, and my
lungs fill with the turbulence
of his passage,
                    down here, between
one solitude and the next, love comes
to this, to nothing but this.

4

THE GARDENER

1:

Arcadio says that tree's called Tree.
That perennial, drooping over its fallen
crimson petals, he calls Permanent.
He can translate the leaves of the bougainvillaea,
the hieroglyphs on the aphid's wing,
the runes the ant inscribes on the honey mesquite.

Walking an intransigent flagstone into place,
ill-favored piece of a clumsy puzzle,
he improvises as he goes, building
a crazy pavement for our shoes.
Green hummingbirds creak like tiny doors
in the fitful breeze.

"The mesquite needs cutting back," he smiles.
Wrestling a thorny, sawed-off
six-foot branch, he tears a spray off the fuschia.
Face down, it's pressing limp, lanceolate
leaves against the bricks while its mother grieves,
tolling her magenta bells.

Now he eases the root-bound patience from her pot
and sets her in a fresh-turned bed (old embers
for new urns), scatters a fistful
of compost from his gunnysack, redistributing
the earth, then bathes her feet.

"We need more earth, señor," Arcadio says.
Three burros of compost, two of loam. He weighs
in his palm a lump of sun-dazed clay, pale, dense,
obdurate as death. In all our books
there is no name for it.

2:

Three mornings a week his key
turns in the lock and sets our day in motion.
Then two enchanted hours exalting the ivy,
exorcising the weeds, rites of the paring knife,
sacraments of bucket and hose.

Coming to say goodbye, he drops
a rosebud on my page, an eloquent period
swathed in moss-green sepals. From the ravaged tip
a corpse-white rose grub cranes,
its lifework likewise interrupted.
"Here's why they do not bloom."

His eyes twin flames of passionate attention,
he turns to take his leave, bearing in his hand
both bud and worm.

3:

He's kneeling in the rain again,
weeding the geraniums,
dividing the waters from the waters,
the darkness from the light.

His smile rides out our protests
like a glistening keel. One drop
winks on his forelock. Bright rivulets
trickle from his fingers toward ecstatic roots.

4:

On his way back with a pocketful of nails
he pauses to reconsider the view—the town

cascading beneath him onto the plateau,
the fields of early corn, the fruitless plains.

He has been training the trumpet vine. Returning,
he spies one impertinent creeper sidling
among the geraniums. Reproachfully,
he tugs it free and stands it against the wall.

Called from his task neither by scorn nor praise,
eyes fixed on the nailhead, utterly
contained within the boundaries of his skin,
he hears his bones ring at the hammer blows.

THE MASON

Sprawled on the kitchen tiles, the mason thrusts
his arm to the shoulder down the ragged hole,
twisting, writhing, groping for a way out.

Furtive emanations found us out,
seeping through crevices under the sink one week
before he came with his chisel to set them free.

"That way." He pointed across the dining room,
his right hand dripping with a dozen years
of inglorious issue, slatternly malefactions.

He knelt to widen the hole. Under the tiles,
brick. Under that, cement. Then he cocked his ear
and tapped his hammer thrice on the thin slate lid,

then once for real. Black fragments toppled into
the steamy soup, splattering the wall,
the sink, the stove, the cabinets, himself.

All we'd consigned to the void, all we'd thought
to put behind us—followed by wads of paper
and gallons of priceless water—leapt from the darkness.

We stroll into the garden, drinking liters
of sweet mountain air while he scoops into a bucket
everything we'd thought to hide. "No problem,"

he says, as he comes out grinning. "All clear now."
He'll bury our squalor in the garden and cover the hole.
Then we can take up where we left off, casting

our secrets out of mind, while the geranium
and the patience wait for the rain in the tremulant shadow,
wait for our leavings to percolate down to their roots.

ARTEMIO AND THE SEÑORA

for Kay

"Do you play the piano, Señora?" Artemio asks,
bowing at the baby grand as he waits to be paid.
"Once, long ago, I knew a girl who played."
His face is a mask hacked by a dull machete,
the mouth a little hole, the nose a knob,
the eyeballs bored with an auger, set with two
obsidian crumbs.

Whoever carved him from whatever stump
must have been thinking of something else at the time.
His arms are of a length, but the clumsy blade
bit down on one palm and sheared off the first three fingers,
leaving thumb and little finger stiffly opposed,
ill-starred lovers, doomed neither to part
nor reconcile.

Despite this (or because of it, who knows),
deep in his heartwood Artemio hides the soul
of an artist. He knows the inmost thoughts of doors.
Holding his makeshift hand like a portable anvil,
the keys he shapes freehand from blanks of brass
are functional and slim as a grasshopper's mandible.
One lies on the piano now, a shining icon
to guard the house.

The Señora weaves an etude on a warp of steel
while Artemio stands in the door like a graceless saint.
Behind the hole in his mask, something is smiling.
Tiny flecks of metal gild his shoes
in the waning light.

MARTA

The sermon wafts above the congregation,
iridescent, perfect, a host of weightless
bubbles, dissipating as they rise.

A score of virtues winks on the lips of the children
shrieking in the churchyard, on the pink ecstatic
tongue of the mongrel lolloping at their heels,

on the infant squalling from the depths of its mother's rebozo
while, in the heart of the tiny chapel,
charity, purity, and piety stream down Marta's

long jet hair and pink tulle *quince años* gown,
down the rosebud border spiralling
from precocious breasts to new spike heels.

Everything—Marta teetering over the cobbles
homeward in the gentle rain,
her mother crouching in the kitchen over the *mole,*

the motley rock group tuning up in the patio
(a dusty chicken-run wreathed in bougainvillaea),
the tranquil goat in the doorway,

the globe of mirrors dangling from the jacaranda,
the fugitive red and green and yellow confetti—
everything bursts on my tongue like melliferous bubbles

as Marta steps over the threshold into the patio
(barnyard, backyard, mud-brick ballroom, whatever)
into the first waltz of her fifteenth year.

THE BUTCHER

Every year, less meat on the butcher's bones
and less in his case. Behind the immaculate glass,
as in a jeweler's window, three cutlets reign.

The less he has, the more it's worth.
Long ago he drove off the last of his customers
with his bloated prices and his haggard scowl.

Today no one comes. A single fly
appraises the cutlets, but he pays no mind.
Standing by his case he gazes out the door

hour on hour. What's he watching for?
His eyes gleam dimly in their hammocks of shadow,
two blue marbles in an orphan's pocket.

SUFFICIENT UNTO THE DAY

And the heavens opened.
Five days of cataracts,
too much, too soon—
before the corn was in.

The water's taken back
the lower field. In the depths
the bean vines quiver, a school
of jade-green minnows.

Halfway through the winter
even the withered stalks
from the upper field will give out
beneath an implacable sky.

And still the ox, running
a contemplative tongue
across his muzzle, munches
the lush new grass.

HERE

Flycatcher's back on his telephone wire
reviewing his troops, calm as a maharajah,
his turban a petal of outrageous geranium.

He sets himself straight with the wind and takes stock.
His sweetheart's preening in the jacaranda
among the dark pods,

and somewhere a canyon wren is calling.
His brief impromptu spills down-scale
like mercury down a flight of crystal stairs.

Clouds have broken, the mesquite's bearded with light.
The sky gleams through for a moment,
a clean-washed ground on which cloud-figures dance.

Nothing but rain, and more rain,
and these shimmering pauses.
My heart's up to here.

SO LONG

The mesquite sadly waves his thousand pods
like parchment-yellow, knobbed, arthritic fingers
in the same breeze that riffles his grey-green beard
as if, for the first time now, he realizes
how enchanting I am in my pale blue bark
and impetuous roots, scurrying aimlessly over
the flagstones like a demented ant, how dull
it will be when I'm gone, with nothing to watch but lizards
and hummingbirds, with nothing to do but snooze
in the August sun, dazed by cicada calls
and Sunday bells, as if only now he sees
how beguiling are my comings-out and goings-in,
how meticulously I vein my cloud-white leaves,
how much he missed me, even while I was here.

❧5❧

WHAT COMES TO A MAN

The evolutionary advantage of having two different minds is obvious; possession of two independent problem solving organs increases mightily the likelihood of a creative solution to a novel problem. At the same time there is an enormous increase in the likelihood of internal conflict. And so we have man, the most innovative of species and at the same time the most at odds with himself.

—Joseph Bogen

Indeed, schizophrenics are almost drowning in sensory data.

—Julian Jaynes

Finkel is Peterson spelled backwards. Sometimes.

—F.A.P.

1 :

After 50 yrs of being unattached what does it take to get together? I remember giving you the right as my alter ego to care on the steps there at 70th & Lex . . . surely now I'm able to join up myselves.

It's Leap Year's Day again,
time for a tiny course correction
to make up for slighted microseconds,
amends for bygone indiscretions.
So I've opened your box,
forget-me-not blue, aswarm
with all your voices, harangue
and incantation, anguish,
panic, waggery.
          Thirteen years
since I stowed it away: your ghost
is capering through my bones
like an impish wind.

Gid called me Pete, even though I was the younger . . . Finkel
called me Pete, recognizing & trusting me, and I thunderstroke
him on the canting stairs.

The right to care
sprang from your lips fully armed,
her derisive smile, her nipples tipped in bronze,
granting me leave to look after you,
then and thereafter, to bear you in mind.
Like being knighted with an icicle:
I still feel in my gizzard
the muffled rumblings of malaise.

       <u>*Nobody here calls me Pete.*</u> *Or even Fratta. Youse is me brudder.*

To sweep up the pieces, to resurrect your selves
(your prodigal ego, your improbable ghost)
from this litter of postcards, letters, photos,
this one-inch slice of your profile
in a clean white shirt and violet tie (untied),
unsmiling, barely acknowledging the lens.
Penciled on the back, one lonely pronoun:
                                You.
Taped to my wall you're scowling down at me,
one long hard look in the mirror.
                       What do you see?

    MY SHIRT IS CLEAN BUT I'M A DIRTY OLD MAN.

§

Ridiculous being the old soak
of the neighborhood. Drunk
and drunk again. Carrying
the ale home. My uncle Sam
brewed it in the bathtub

every Sunday between services.
He was sweet and how sweet
his house smelled. Uncle Sam
was a sweet smelling uncle.
When my father caught me he
would retch me. He didn't
drink. Uncle Sam and I buried
him and went to his house and drank.

A silent butler you called him, over brislings and beer,
a shabby despot, a brooding sanctimonious Swede,
buttling while Mama baked the cassoulet.

One queasy afternoon in the living room
he pressed the smoldering bowl of his pipe
against your thigh—a gesture of affection.

An unaccountable rictus disfigured his lips,
half buffoonery, half malice. Too bad
the old fraud couldn't stay buried for good.

After hours, lumbering homeward
(any port in a maelstrom) you keep
an eye on your shoes, the left, the right,
reassuringly reappearing
on solid pavement—the lip of the vortex
only a stumble away.
                    I've learned
long since to look the other way.

            Sooner or later we all fall in.

*To whom does a man impart his music and his laughter?—to
his kind . . . Imagine, I never learned that simple thing, nor
that my Andromeda was not millions of light years away but
right here.*

Fishing your fathomless babble this morning, I snagged
three billets-doux from a single day in Laredo.
In the second screed you're knocking on your coffin.

*I have made my peace. My mind is at one with man and his
universe . . . I do not panic this time, what strength is needed
I hope I have to leave you the memory of a man.*

What an arduous craft you've chosen for yourselves,
salvaging the engrams grain by grain.
By the last dispatch, old ghost, you're in full cry.

*Talk about Damascus road Saul or Boehme or Fox or W. Blake.
I'm getting damn close to picking up my bed & walking.*

*Could it be possible that even under the schiz I am a thorough
wrong-o?*

I dream you back tonight, undaunted wrong-o,
sleepwalking the perilous alleys of Laredo,
weaving across the interstellar bridge
between Damascus and Andromeda.

Chained to her windy wheel, Andromeda's
plunging headlong toward you, arms outstretched,
but you're lurching for Damascus once again,
blind as a pie-eyed saint—and your back is turned.

The trouble was you didn't know me.
A punk kid with mumps sitting on
the window-sill when you took
your leap. Fourth floor was it?

But you had a good cat. The cat
descended. And the patterned china.
The cutlery cascaded. The sun shone.
You shouldn't have done that
to a kid with the mumps.

After your cat licked your stalking
bloody face turbulence came up
and hit me in the mumps. Now
your cat is my cat.

Back-door boy, killing time in a stranger's kitchen,
between two provinces, inhabiting neither.
Summers at the Master's country house,
drifting the vast lawns dappled with dandelions,
angling off the rocks with a hand line and a can
of periwinkles.
            You took me back and showed me how,
played uncle to my neophyte. Toward dusk
we built ourselves a little ring of stones
and sizzled our mingy catch on a driftwood fire.

That was the best of it, sitting
there in the dark. Waiting, not
for the eels, but the moon
on the rocks; the slow talk.
The pipes. The sea sloshing.
Pants wet, cold in Summer.
We spoke to one another.
The line tightening on the ebb.

What I'm trying to say is "You look over my shoulder while I
look over yours."

Life depends on loony intersections.
Lost in my own maze, I blundered on yours.
Nights at Lenox & 112th,
swapping small talk with off-duty whores,
the heathen Swede and the unregenerate Jew.
Mornings-after at the zoo, watching
the tiger pace his seamless figure 8,
that desperately elegant swerve at the wall—
infinity in a dismal ten-foot cage.

Midsummer Sunday drinking by the lake.
Creak of oarlocks: the couples were rowing in concert
round the bend. The park, a frazzled carpet
three miles long, lay gasping under a steel-blue ceiling.

Kneeling at the brink, a fledgling skipper
plied his half-pint argosy into the breeze, then with it,
world without end, as the lubberly afternoon
groaned on its axle grudgingly duskward.

Two fugitive rhapsodes on an alien shore,
shoulder to shoulder on the boathouse steps,
we hoisted our sweaty bottlenecks aloft
and downed another toast to the muse of water.

2:

How the hell did I get here? 1942.
Sgt. of cryptology, strapped .45, armed escort.
Chambered and on my rounds.
How harrowing, how infinite those rounds,
pacing a radio room in Panama
while the good earth self-destructed at both ends.
How fearfully sweet it was to speak in tongues.

Yet how ill-favored, half a lifetime later,
seven remorseless years in durance vile,
pacing the wind-bitten wards of Atlantic City,
haunting Boardwalk, never passing Go.

§

All things past yabber and yowl
on this spitted sand. Bump, staw
and rackle me. I am unstudy
grizzled by the long chime of the tide.

On your perpetual expedition to the sea,
barefoot as a pilgrim, toting your shoes,
you pause on the still-damp sand at the lip of the tide
watching the breakers topple and reassemble.

At your feet the vagrant weed dreams
between voyages. The sea-wind scours your eyes
as a lone gull settles to his feast of leavings.
Brushing the sand from your soles, you resume your shoes.

Stalking the empty boardwalk, transient as seaweed,
keen as the gull, intrepid, eerily free,
you've weathered the worst.
February

winks like a lizard and vanishes,
leaving its tail in your hand.

§

Trudging through the umbrage
from clearing to clearing,
you know the forest
like the back of your neck.

Wherever you turn
black oak and bitternut
leer down like a clan
of malevolent fathers.

Rinsing your soles
in the ebb tide this evening
you hear them behind you
chuckling and snickering.

> *Well, there it is, friend. Help me, father, do not hate me so . . .*
> *Do not let me die, father.*

§

In the ancient, perpetual war between the self
and the non-self, there's enmity everywhere.
Young blacks cruising the boulevards
in battered Cadillacs, old Jews debouching
from storefront synagogues in green-black overcoats
and Assyrian beards—squatters, parvenus,
barbarous, suspect, unaccountable.

Nor are they always simple to distinguish
from noncombatants. Even the dust is a stranger,
crowding every aperture. Any moment

some fanatical antibody might trigger a massacre:
transports of savagery, spasms of slaughter.

Under a mountain of outworn inventions
warriors are sleeping (imperturbable torpor,
shoulders lapped in epaulets of dust)
while deep in the bowels of the city a shadow
slips from a doorway cradling a burden—
a weapon, an infant, a bundle of rags.
A baffled sentry bawls out, "Who goes there?"

§

*A couple embracing on the beach this morning. Like being hit
in the groin with an axe handle. Slewing around & almost
going to my knees. I doubt that this was a put up job, but . . .*

They're throwing a party upstairs.
You can hear it carom off the walls
and seep through your sweat-streaked ceiling.
Fretful as a splinter, you ache
to join the party, senator from the state
of dislocation, your infinitesimal
pressure against history faint as starlight
thrumming the hairs on a general's wrist.

Climbing from your cold-water grotto,
you bob through the flotsam,
fetch up on a stool by the anchovies.
A mermaid stoops to inquire: *What do you do?*
Her baubles dangle in the weedy shadow.

I feed on air, you smile, *like an orchid.
I do with, my delectable sea grape,
I do without.*

3:

Guess I'm boring you but you're the only one I can talk to. I
am sick of lying around here. I am angry at myself for not get-
ting involved . . . I am angry at myself for listening to voices.

In the beginning were the voices,
ranting, commanding, admonishing, mocking—
every mudlark had his own,
begotten and died in him.

Now the hour's come round again
to hang on the lips of the dead,
but the sibyl's gone stone deaf,
the oracle's got a bone in his throat.

And who's that jamming the traffic
with flutter and wow—is it the old ones
gibbering in their crypts?
Doom glances off their hides like April rain.

A man with more country than you can bear,
mired in it up to your thalamus while the alley
seethes with strangers after your giblets for any
number of crimes you never remember committing.
Sure enough, under your window

a clutch of kids go by chanting Bell, bell. Tolling, you know.
And on the subway—Pete's dead, Pete's dead.

Every grunt, every whimper from without or within
demands your attention, complete and immediate,
a deluge of premonitions, portents, auguries
and, every now and again, a niggardly respite
in some foul backwater, doing the dead man's float.

If "they" get or have gotten to you——& why are "they" so afraid
and hating?——and who are "they"?

How much easier is it, up to your ears in beer?

Do you mean this "conspiracy at the top" is my own brain?

§

Get up you wretched old SOB & look the world in the eyes.

Across Baltic in the P.O. parking lot
the mailmen's Pintos line up at the fence
to watch you pass. The Grand Old Flag
droops on its tall white stalk like a wilted flower.

By the long green windowless hotels,
swathed against sparrows, the seeded lawns
thrust glass-green spicules through their bandages.
From the schoolyard tiny screams pierce morning's shawl.

It's a bad day on Atlantic Avenue——and still
it's the only game in town. A bent black yard man
raking dead leaves from the privet meets
the ghost of your smile with a spectral grin.
While the sun hums overhead to the rustle of money,
he scoops up his old bones and shakes them again.

§

You know I am not so hard headed or hearted as not to beg a
thousand humble pardons of those I've offended. But to whom
do I address them?

Drunk or sober, every night, wherever you are,
you empty your pockets onto the dresser:
billfold, penknife, loose change, keys, revealed——

to whom? this laying-out of your resources:
Look, whoever you are, this is all I possess.

> *No, really, this is beyond ludicrous imaginings. I can't believe*
> *it most of the time. Who, me?*

> *Partial fog, rain spatter, onshore breeze, people on the beach*
> *getting rheumatiz & sunburn. Well, what isn't poetry?*

You take the cold way home along the boardwalk
in the brackish, gaunt Atlantic City dawn.
Beside you in the somnolent casinos
the wheels turn dreamily on seagreen tables,
brigades of one-armed bandits hold up morning.

The sea wind kisses you fiercely, leaving on your lips
the smack of straining rope, of creaking holds,
astringent, keen, a penny for the helmsman,
sour as recollection, shrewd as doubt,
dank as your mother's brow in the midnight ward.

To make good your losses, replenish the waters,
your daily brine. You run the tip of your tongue
across the knife-edge of your smile to take it in.

Breakfast over, you're pondering
the back of your cereal box:
CUT ALONG DOTTED LINE AND SAVE.
Down to the last of the instant,
you pick up the scissors
and kneel, rapt as a saint,
to sever your corroded

soles from the linoleum,
then drift to the window
unencumbered, unconditional,
alone.

       Of course, that I'm nuts is not here to the point, but true, too.

§

       Tonight burned crab cakes. Drunk & horny. Old friend, I'll call
       you Pete, you call me Fingal.

Deep in the abyss, a few synapses sing
to one another. Somewhere another ego's
taking shape.

Two minds in you. Now two in me,
yabber and yowling—
your mind unfurling, leafing out in mine.

How nice that somewhere
there's an alter ego
for every altered one.

4:

       How can a woman be so beautiful
       and not love me? Expel my lungs,
       say hello to her. Huzzah, the eyes
       are not blue, the hair is not blonde,
       the ankles thick or no. See the expression
       loving me. Come now I want you. All
       ways and always. I love you.

       Tomorrow my name is yours.

In the newspaper tonight, it's as you thought:

> *The mole has no mating call, though it can make a couple of*
> *sounds that are more or less "conversational."*

Contemplating the peacock's wanton scream,
you home in on the great whale's shameless serenade
throbbing halfway round the world. A mole of few words,
you plunge through the small talk:

> *. . . these small sounds probably occur when a male and a*
> *female mole stumble into one another.*

Somewhere a soft grey nymph with moist myopic eyes
dogpaddles toward you through the fragrant loam.
This very moment, the earth might crumble between you,
the last crumbs of topsoil toppling from her velvet nose.

§

> *Saw Jupiter & Venus in the Eastern sky this morning . . . pin*
> *oaks holding out . . .*

Outside your window, the pin oak's long-dead leaves
twirl from her bony fingers,
a swarm of zombie dancers doing the waltz macabre.

Shuffling past, an old man skewers
a leaflet of yesterday's news
and thrusts it into his sack, unread.

§

Grey squirrel's clambering his black lattice,
branch to branch across the haggard evening.
As one branch succumbs to the gravity of his need,

another reaches hungrily after him, quivering.
Stone cold at the bottom of winter,
at the end of his rope, it's either up or out,

while there in your furnished eyrie, the weather's
windless, stifling, static, though a barely
discernible charge accumulates in the carpet—

until one clumsy touch might set it ablaze.

§

I know I've been bugging you people with cards & letters,
maybe less now that I have a plant (I bought myself one) to
say "goodnight" to.

Under the thin chill rippling light of the Miller
High Life sign your hands show their true colors,
as into the peaceful sleeves of your windbreaker
the blood withdraws. Astraddle your teetering bar stool
you feel it thrumming the chambers of your heart.

By the dim gazebo in the park your favorite maple
drains the cool green liquor from her leaves
and leaves them empty, revealing aboriginal madders,
parched oranges. You're fixing to drop both hands
at the feet of the provident nymph in the vermilion mini
nursing her double bourbon like a warm brown baby.

§

I have just now come around. I'll be on the wagon for months
now what with the change in the weather . . .

Bone dry, half past midnight, the boardwalk's yours,
leaning on the stern rail, eternal tourist,

watching the tide retreat. Pensive, grave,
well caffeinated, you can feel your dendrites twitter.
You've come for the sea cure, the salt cure,
drying out by the briny (dominion of the moist,
fecund, treacherous), your weather eye keen
as the edge of the nail-paring moon.
                                    You could
amble out forever on those glimmering flats.
You can hear the ebb tide whispering, *Keep in touch.*

§

> *Been taking coffee with a fellow schiz named Patterson. (I say
> taking because "drinking" reminds me of beer.). He pretends not
> to understand my words but I think he's putting me on. Good
> fellow. Your children can start calling me Uncle again.*

You come bearing a cluster of subway posies,
vagrant, avuncular, perpetual uncle.
Rapt nephews bring you ale in golden cans,
nieces wear your pop-tops for sweetheart rings.

At Sunday brunch with your cold war buddy,
bottom feeding in the gene pool,
you nuzzle the dregs like a golden carp.

§

> *Not that I can have her really, twice married and three kids
> . . . And I do love this woman, heaven help me. So I may move
> on . . . because what can be fruitful? For either of us.*

She wakes to hear you barking in your room,
whom she took in last month like a homeless pooch,
who only yesterday stood on his own hind legs,

70

stone cold sober, drying the dinner dishes,
praising her sea-blue eyes in broken Swedish—
howling now at a pack of nightmare mailmen,
nobody's dog, gnawing the children's sleep,
his leash, the last threads of her endurance.

§

> . . . *feel like a bird, not a dodo or moa, nor a running bird, an*
> *ostrich or rhea, but flightless like a kiwi.*

Sunday morning, slumped on your usual pew,
attending the pin oak's shy quadrille with her shadow
on their grassy, turd-bespangled dancing floor,
the amazons strolling their dobermans, a detachment
of semi-detachable widows marching into April,
you consider breaking off a piece for yourself.

By the relentless heroism of solitude almost undone
you anatomize the enchantments of marriage,
the raptures of coupling, beatitudes of pin and screw.
Beside you one gilt leaf leaps from the pin oak's wrist
from which it has been clinging winter long.
Twirling, she curtseys to the newborn grass
and flags the first gust passing, north or west.

§

> *Still slogging in the foothills checking equipment, experi-*
> *menting, lining up personnel . . . Guides, pack animals, all set*
> *for propitious weather—which happens every morning.*

Time unrolls at our feet,
a bolt of ragged carpet,
dwindling. We feel on our napes
the icy breath of our forebears.

We needn't turn, we know
that bleak, myopic gaze.
We're a shortlived tribe, with a taste
for tribute and a roaring thirst for praise.

We bow out one by one
in a burst of applause and a cloud
of incomprehension, still
in the foothills of understanding.

5:

> I must tell you. The biopsy is cancer. The whole head, ears,
> eyes, noses & throats. I nap. I believe the docs want radiation
> & chemo. The board meets Tuesday, what other decision can
> <u>they</u> make . . . I don't know what decision buys me optimum
> time. What would I do with it?

After a cryptic three-year silence.
Where had you gone to earth, amigo?
And where in the world (in your dogged safari
from 70th & Lex to Ward 5E) did you savor
that one last gobbet of optimum time?

> Not so bad in Spring at the foot of the moraine. Follow the
> melt, eat salmon. . . . Take a Labrador squaw, wander South to
> the trees, start again. Go West. Plenty of practice, a knowing
> axe.

§

> Where are my people? Youse?

When the rivers return to their sources,
when the leaves fly home to their forsaken branches,
when the gypsies go back where they came from,

when the killer revisits the scenes of his innocence,
you'll wriggle back to your mère
in her seaweed housecoat and shipwreck slippers.
You'll dig up an almanac of weeds, and trace your roots.

Till then you'll persist in your one-man diaspora,
tramping the boondocks with suitcase and six pack
from wilderness to wilderness,
catching your breath in the villainous cities,
snoring fitfully in rented sheets.
If people had roots they'd roost like trees
up to their ankles in earth.
They'd shuck their rags when the north wind called.

§

What is it they want of me, Uncle,
the insatiable dead?
Are they unconversable as ever?

I hunch here spilling words into the grave
in lieu of ram's blood:
Listen, whoever you are: these are all I have.

§

      *I have sailed from Aiaia; I no longer dine at Circe's table. It's
      a long way to Ithaca.*

The stewardess leans from the aisle to tuck you in.
Your nostrils quail in a gust of maternal perfume.
You waft a thankyou back.
                    She'll return with a cart
of complimentary headphones and iced libations.
The angel of bourbon will press her beautiful thumbs

against your temples. Dvorak will drip like glucose
down the chaste grey vinyl to comfort the company—
seventy breathless celebrants strapped in their pews,
skimming the shingles of oblivion.

> *There is a yoga exercise that produces a full mental direction*
> *allowing free passage in or out. That is, compartments are*
> *integrated, resistance flux dissipated, force fields lowered . . .*
> *Anyway, does this mean anything to you?*

Where are you now——still drifting?
a cell without a country
bobbing the arteries of Megalopolis
looking for somewhere harmless to happen?

You pass through airport x-ray portals
like a cosmic particle, passing
roadblocks and customs agents,
a gypsy meson, biding nowhere long.

In a flyblown harbor bar in Vera Cruz
you soak your ID card in sweet white wine,
reload your empties with lullabies to mermaids,
send obscene postcards to the editors of *Time*.

> *If I didn't care enough, why should you? Whatever happens is*
> *what comes to a man——all my fault, what the hell.*

I care by rights, old mole. I know what happens—
each man jack cast buck-naked on a moonstruck shingle.
What comes after, the spared call history.

Your last farewell: an aerial postcard view
of the Philly Hilton, eighteen stories high
for a headstone, with your epitaph on the back.

> *Next week transferred . . . don't*
> *know proper address.*
> *See you*

Then nothing but my own stillborn farewell,
still sealed, hand-stamped DECEASED: RETURN
TO SENDER. Well, I'm sending it back with interest.

Have you made it past the foothills, doppelganger?
Have you run across that crack in circumstance
a naked soul might slip through, sooner or later?

You had one thing right for sure, in any case—
I see you peering out from every mirror.
Faintly of course, but clearer every day.

6

WAITING FOR A HEART

1:

To the living, the words for death are like the dead.
When they come calling, they're difficult to make out,
ragged at the edges, unaccountable ghosts,
voices hoarse and thin with long disuse.

To the dying, the words for life evoke the same
uncanny shudder. Once the word *endure*
had fire in her eyes, strode so firmly
across the boards of morning, they groaned at her passage.

Now at night she whimpers in the corridor.
Someone calls timidly, but she won't come in.

2:

Someone floats on his back as the current bears him,
some seasons bobbing on arctic calms, timeless, numb,
some seasons basking on incandescent sands,
would send a postcard, but he's out of stamps.

And what should he write? *The weather's here.*
Wish I were fine? A new language is needed,
compounded almost entirely of verbs
and prepositions, vast and languorous
as whales. A language untroubled by nouns, without
person or tense, one gender, and infinite moods.

From time to time the room reappears. The same room,
yet always a different face, dangling just out of reach
like some gross, amorphous fruit better left untasted.

3:

Having finished shaving Someone's grizzled beard,
the nurse holds up a mirror. Doesn't that look younger?
Immersed in his own dissolution, he's too busy to look,
see what his children see. Between him and them
an unbridgeable chasm widens with every wheeze
of the breathing machine.

When was it otherwise? With every year,
as he changed before their eyes from a god to a man
to a walking fossil, it grew progressively wider, whereas
from his perspective it was they who withdrew
while he remained where (and whatever it was)
he had always been.

4:

The breathing machine
can only breathe.

Someone, too, was once a machine
for breathing. Ingenious:
the inspiration, the expiration.

Together now, the two of them
can only breathe. The little breaths
follow one another like lemmings, tumbling
over the edge into emptiness.

Not one reaches out
with its tiny paws
to scrabble the silence.
No small talk, no
faltering song.

5:

Someone else is walking round a corner,
trundling his heart like a kilo
of rib roast home from market.

Or driving out of the city,
nestled in the bosom of his Buick,
thrumming to heavy metal.

Someone bored, inching
nearer, nearer to the edge
with Someone's heart in his hands.

Someone uncomprehending,
blissful, doomed, who doesn't
need to see Someone hovering,

heartlessly waiting ahead.

BURNT UMBER STUDY

It's a jungle out there
in my neighbor's garden.
His vines molest the rose
through the cyclone fence.

Outside my kitchen window
one scraggly branch
snores in the afternoon
like a dried-out wino.

This windowpane has been
through hell and home,
yet how calmly it stands here
attending the sunset.

Two clouds come sailing in
like enormous nurses
bearing jug upon jug
of heavenly rain.

BIDDEFORD POOL

1:

To the north lies the pool itself, a tidal basin that is nearly drowned at low water and almost closed by a mile-long spit of sand.

    —J. M. Collins and J. E. McCarthy, Nature Walks in Southern Maine

Dead ahead Gooseberry Island
breaches like a whale of slate.
That stunted knuckle to its left
was once the penultimate stop
on the underground, carrying
slaves to Canada. And there,
past the lip of the shingle,
in the undertow, the elegant
metamorphs tumble, thumbing
the lexicon of stone.
               The swells
ride widdershins, churning the cobbles,
erratic gravel, reluctant emigrants
borne off by the imperious ice,
stray souvenirs she picked up on the way.

Now over the headland, at the tip of this flimsy
finger of seacoast the continent crooks
at the insolent sea—a halo of sea gulls.
Asquint in the wind, her icy kiss,
the smack of stolen tears.

2:

. . . the bobbing gulls, rising and then dropping again as the swell moves past, prove that it is the form of the swell, not the water itself, that is moving.

    —David Kendall, Glaciers and Granite

Somewhere out there, beneath the gulls,
a drowned moraine lies.
                              Eons ago the ice,
retreating, wept into the greedy sea,
the continent stretched in his bed and rose.
And the sea likewise, nuzzling the emigrants
onto the shingle.
                    At the brink
life clings: rockweed, limpet, periwinkle.

While, abandoned, groaning as they roll,
a commonwealth of cobbles, naked,
friable, diffident, lapidary,
battering each other into shape
toward this extravagance, this lovely
rubble, haunted by gleaners
                              to satisfy
what hunger, compensate what loss?

AT ROXY'S TOPLESS

for Cinnamon

Because she chortled like a sibyl at my question,
perched naked as a number on the edge of the table,
smoothing the wadded dollars, singing through
the din and the scrimmage: "Maine!"
                                        because
she recited "Wild nights! Wild nights!" like a schoolgirl
in the thundering disco, through the drunken
crackers' whoop and the clang of their galvanized ashtrays
against the tables at Roxy's Topless,
                                        because
I felt round my thighs the chill of the surf she rose from,
the salt in my wounds, the languor of deliverance,
did that yield me the luxury to dream her
somewhere else—shopping for chicken thighs at the super?
checking out Trollope novels from the local library?
Blasphemy. Like wrestling the Blessed Virgin
down from her altar into the local K-Mart, to strand her
in Housewares or in Beauty Aids.
                            "Ah! the sea!
Might I but moor / Tonight in thee"—body
of a schoolgirl, slim arms wrapped round the backs
of her knees, thighs parted in a transcendent V,
her sequinned pubes flaring an inch from my face
among the crumpled singles—her offerings!
rapt as a cat among wind-scattered leaves.

THE KINDLY ONES

Streaming from Erebus through a crack in the pavement
they crowd the door to the abortion clinic.
Older than Zeus, in Ilium every beggar had one
to keep him honest. Under their lavender pantsuits
coal-black breasts, bat wings, leathery shanks,
thorny scourges in their turquoise purses
to chasten the prodigals sidling to slaughter.

Among us as ever they chide the infanticides
past the threshold of shadows brandishing
blissful conviction and raspberry smiles, counseling
chastity, poverty, a term of virtuous labor,
then age on age of sackcloth and vain remorse.

MOVING DAY

No paintings
only naked places
where the paintings hung.

No silence either.
Our voices ricochet off the walls
like capering puppies.

And no regrets.
Some magnanimous hand's
unsnapping my leash.

Let's ride up front with the moving men,
our snoots out the window
snuffling the ambrosial freeway breeze.

GETTING THE MESSAGE

Laurel and hellebore, bull's blood, blood of the lamb,
essence of aconite, fumes of prophecy,
whatever Earth herself might drink, the sibyl
swallows, quaffing the coo-roo of doves,
the rustle of oak leaves, sighs of the sightless dead,
inhaling whole days of knucklebones and entrails,
awakening slowly, cautiously, temples throbbing—
lingering on her tongue, the dregs of dream.

Whereas, in the cave of Trophonius in Boeotia,
it is the supplicant who gets the message.
After three days of purification, knocking back
the waters of forgetfulness and the waters of memory,
herded by two boys down the path to the river,
drenched and anointed, decked in a linen tunic
and the fillets of sacrifice, clutching in each hand
a honey cake, he descends the oracular chasm—
to be dragged feet first through a narrow hole in the floor.
"There in the darkness" (at least according to Plutarch)
"a blow falls on his skull so he seems to die."

Returned to the light feet foremost, minus his cakes,
steered by a priest to the Throne of Mnemosyne,
told to repeat whatever it was he heard,
the supplicant stutters and mumbles like an imbecile.
(Who knows what he tasted there in the womb of Earth,
what dripped from the groin of darkness onto his brow,
what sibilant whispers rinsed his inmost ear?)
He recalls round his ankles the clammy hands of water,
harks back to that whiff of suspicion at the foot of the path.
"Then, still in a dazed condition," Plutarch assures us,
"he is hauled once more to the Altar of Good Fortune
where he regains his senses and the power to laugh."

THE PHRYGIAN VERSION

According to the Greeks, Athena fashioned the flute
from the shinbone of a stag. Blowing into it
by the bank of the Hippocrene, she caught a glimpse
of her face, lips puckered like a pigskin purse,
and pitched the wretched tibia into the creek,
where that satyr Marsyas was sure to look,
shambling to slake his morning-after thirst.
Befuddled by those other-worldly wails
cascading from the cursed bone, his face in the water—
pug-nose and ragged ears—seemed ugly as ever.
Foul airs, unseemly figures assailed Apollo's
fastidious ear, and the inevitable followed.

The Athenians swear to us the end was clean,
the edge of Apollo's anger scalpel-thin.
One stroke, scrotum to throat—and lo!
kneeling, the deity peeled back the belly-fleece,
parting that downy sheath, as when the breeze
draws back a cloud and aether blazes through.

The Phrygians, however, those shameless queens,
those tricked-out trollops reeking of cheap cologne,
tell us their great-great-grandfathers long before
were shagged from nape to heel with caprid hair.
To hear their side of it, a kid called Marsyas,
haunting the fetid pond where the centaurs drank
(attar of donkey-piss and trampled moss),
caught the breeze playing with herself in the reeds,
tore out a handful and capered back to his lair.
Interval: from the mouth of the grotto flowed
the first uncertain half-notes, hesitant tremolos.

No reasonable Greek would dream a goat
could bleat in counterpoint, some unkempt brute

could teach their bards to sing. To hear them talk,
their proto-poet wriggled fully crowned
from the cool, tall, smooth, Euclidean brow
of that maiden aunt, Athena of the withering look.

And still, the Phrygians sneer, to this very day
no decent Greek can hear the squeal of flutes
and not feel at the nape of his neck the prickling furze.
Before daft Marsyas came, the deities
shuffled cheerlessly their haunts—Chronos
the tone-deaf, dumb Gaia, inarticulate Zeus,
Apollo Pussyfoot, glum as a judge. Up there
no one played anything, not even the air.

THE INCOMPARABLE OATES

(On the fateful return journey from the South Pole, realizing that in his crippled condition he was nothing but a burden to his companions, Captain Lawrence Oates, known in life as Soldier and after death as "the Incomparable," slipped from the tent to his death in a blizzard. The quotations, but for one, are from Scott's journal.)

1:

He slept through the night before last, hoping not to wake—

> Nine hours limping at the end of his rope
> on rotten, black, oblivious stumps, behind
> the three of them, hunched in their harnesses,
> grunting, sweating, half man, half beast—snow crystals
> fixed in their tracks, snagging the runners,
> a third of the Barrier still to go.
>
> Nine hours steaming in his parka,
> thirty-seven below, the wind at his back,
> nine hours beyond pain, asleep on his feet,
> dreaming himself back home again in the stables,
> lulled by the ever-comforting snort of the ponies,
> heady with horse-piss and fresh-laid straw—

but he woke.

2:

> *. . . one person must desire to be sacrificed—in order to profit thereby, the rest must be willing to remember him forever, making him "immortal"—*
>
> —*Mircea Eliade,* Myth and Reality

> A beggarly sacrifice, in any event.
> Not the lithe exemplar climbing the pyramid
> into the blinding light, but the wounded stag

abandoning himself to the jackals' teeth,
not in triumph but in resignation,
hardly "immortal," merely "incomparable,"
braced at the tent flap, gazing into the blizzard.
What profit? one wonders. And who will be left to remember?

3:

He did not—would not—give up hope till the very end. He was a brave soul. This was the end.

Serene in the three-man sleeping bag, between
those two thieves, hope and fortitude,
Blue-eyed Bill and Old Reliable Birdie,
Scott fumbled the pencil in his dead-black fingers,
scribbling to the end this dubious jetsam,
driftwood glyphs, serifs of bladderwrack,
kelp graffiti cast on the shelving page.

4:

Oates' last thoughts were of his mother.

Who knew what passed for thought as Soldier slipped
through the tent flap, muttering over his shoulder,
 "I'm just going outside and may be some time"?
What passed for time as he hobbled into the storm?
What passed for hope at thirty-seven below,
the wind for a comforter, the snow for a pillow?

When they brought his diary to her, his mother
dropped it into the fire, unread. No bells
no cannon rolls, no muffled drums. More like
white noise, a drift of ash on Mother's hearth.

A DAY

Imperturbable languor, placid as talc,
tranquil as a housefly buzzing a puddle of sunlight.
A wintry silence vitrifies the bistro
down to the moth-grey smoke that purls
from the old bookkeeper's meerschaum—

                           almost as if
an eon from now some famished gatherer might
turn up a shard of it with her digging stick,
still glinting in the radioactive sun,
one last communiqué before the silence
crystallized us.

                 Then a waiter coughs,
a news truck rattles past in the midnight street,
shattering the fragile truce like a pane of glass,
and the old man groans to his feet and calls it a day.